Proper Spanish Tapas

THE TRADITIONAL RECIPES

Stephen Lean

First Published 2015
Published by Stephen Lean

Proper Spanish Tapas / Stephen Lean
ISBN: 1508433771
ISBN-13: 978-1508433774

Contents

DEDICATED TO LOVERS OF GOOD FOOD

Take a minute, turn off your phone... listen
Sit back, relax, smile a while... breathe

Now you are ready to enjoy your tapas,
prepared and served the Spanish way:
with soul, with flair and with passion

And, most importantly of all,
with the people you love

"Eating is not merely a material pleasure. Eating well gives a spectacular joy to life and contributes immensely to goodwill and happy companionship. It is of great importance to the morale."

—ELSA SCHIAPARELLI

[1]

Introduction

WHEREVER YOU GO in Spain you will find lively and noisy bars serving tapas, the small plates of superb flavours and local delicacies which epitomise the Spanish way of life.

In its most basic form traditional tapas is simply a small snack or appetiser taken with a drink or two at lunchtime or in the early evening before the main meal. It is essentially a style of eating rather than a form of cooking. Tapas means sociability, friends and family.

Now, throughout the world, tapas will give you a tasty little mouthful of the real Spain without having to jump on an aeroplane to enjoy it!

Tapas has become a popular and healthy addition to the many food styles and cuisines available to us today. Everyone is joining in and realising how pleasurable eating in this way can be. And why not? When you begin to see the sheer range of flavours available you will, I'm sure, want to find out more about 'the small plate with the BIG flavour'.

Wherever you live, you can bring a little Spanish sunshine right into your own home - right now! From an exotic, spicy Moorish dish, to a classic tortilla, to a simple bowl of olives, the choice is entirely yours. But oh, what a choice it is!

The aim of this book is simple: to introduce you to the preparation, cooking and serving of the enormously varied traditional tapas recipes of Spain. I hope you will find the information and recipes herein fun, informative and easy to follow.

Tapas means keeping it simple

Spanish food, and especially tapas, is based on simple methods and the imaginative use of seasonal vegetables and local ingredients. Tapas is essentially hearty and unpretentious. Ingredients are fresh, flavours are robust and recipes are easy. Preparation and presentation is generally pretty straightforward.

You'll find no 'pan-seared' this and 'sun-blushed' that here, my friend. The success of a tapas dish is purely down to one basic criteria: whether or not it tastes good. Which is, I hope you'll agree, the only way it should be.

Tapas means friends and family

You can keep it simple or you can make it as complicated as you like. But whichever way you prefer it, tapas is best served with an early evening drink among friends and lively company. You will not, I promise you, find a more pleasurable and flavour-filled experience anywhere in the world.

So pour yourself a drink, sit back, take your time and enjoy your Spanish tapas to the full. There is no better way to sample the real essence of Spain's lifestyle and culture.

Tapas recipes are as varied and interesting as the people who invented them. The wonderful thing about tapas is that it's food from the heart, to be enjoyed with friends. So if you don't have a specific ingredient don't get too uptight about it, just use something else - they'll still love you for it!

If you can read, you can cook!

This recipe book is not supposed to be a beginner's cookery course! I am assuming that you have some knowledge of cooking and can find your way around the kitchen. However, most of these tapas recipes are so simple that, as my dear mum always used to say: "If you can read it, you can cook it!"

Don't worry about getting everything perfectly to the ounce, measurements are only a guideline. A bit of this, a slosh of that and a glug of the other works just as well.

There is no 'standard' tapas recipe for any individual dish. A simple tortilla, the quintessential omelette, will have a different recipe in every region you may care to visit.

As a rule, tapas means small. The best way to enjoy it is as an aperitif with a glass of fino sherry, a good wine or a cold beer. However, tapas are so versatile that many people make a complete meal of them. These are called 'raciones' and are available everywhere you find tapas. It's the same thing - only bigger.

The main thing is to enjoy yourself and discover new ways with food and recipes, cooked and served the Spanish way: with soul, with flair and with passion. But, most importantly of all, with the people you love.

[2]

Ingredients

TO MAKE THE MOST of your recipes, you will need a selection of the following common ingredients stashed away in your larder cupboard. That way you will always have the basics to rustle up something quick when friends come a-calling.

Store-cupboard basics

OLIVE OIL: Just about the most important ingredient in all tapas dishes. Use the best extra-virgin for dressings and all recipes that call for 'drizzles' of oil. A lesser oil is fine for frying but get a good flavoursome one if you can.

OLIVES: These again are hugely important to tapas. They basically come in three main types: green, coloured and black. They are all, however, products of the same tree.

Green ones are produced from fruits harvested during the ripening period once they have reached normal size but before they change colour.

Coloured ones are produced from reddish or brown coloured fruits harvested when they are completely ripe.

Black ones are produced from fruits which are actually over-ripe and have been darkened by oxidation.

You can use olives in hundreds of dishes and recipes, from the simplest tapas to the most complex cookery. You can put them in salads, serve them with fish and meat, and slice them onto your pizza. You can stuff them, chop them, mince them or just eat them whole with a glass of sherry. You name it and you can probably do it with an olive!

SERRANO HAM (JAMÓN): The best known Spanish ham is Jamón Serrano and the best Jamón Serrano comes from the black Iberian pig fed on acorns. This is known as Jamón Ibérico de Bellota. It's very expensive, but until you've tried it you won't know what you're missing.

Choosing serrano ham is the easy bit. You can buy it by the slice, by the kilo or buy the whole leg - it's up to your personal taste and the depth of your pocket!

There is no difference in quality between a slice of serrano or a whole ham - as long as you buy it from a reputable supplier who knows how to keep it properly and ensures that the carved hams don't dry out.

CHEESE: Spain produces many different cheeses but Manchego is the most well-known and widely-available. It can be anything from soft-ish and mild to strong, nutty and hard.

There are two types of Manchego cheese: the artisanal (farmhouse) type which is made with unpasteurized milk, and the commercial type made with pasteurized milk. Both are available either semi-cured or cured.

To be classed as a genuine Manchego, the cheese must be made from whole sheep's milk from the Manchega sheep which are bred and reared in the region of Castillo La Mancha

GARLIC: Need I say more?! The younger, fresher and juicier, the better.

ONIONS: Spanish onions range from sweet and mild to strong and pungent. Just use whatever you've got.

CHORIZO: The most widely-available chorizos are fully dry-cured and can be eaten without cooking. They are available either picante (hot) or dulce (mild and sweet).

The best chorizos are again made from the Iberian pig and are called, you've guessed it, Chorizo Ibérico. These can contain up to 95% pork with the remainder being made up from pork fat, salt, garlic and paprika. It is the paprika which give them their characteristic red colour.

The other type of chorizo, which has be to cooked, is found in stews and in bean and potato dishes. These chorizos are shorter and come joined together just like your normal sausages.

ALMONDS: A pack or two of whole almonds, either au natural or blanched and skinned.

CHILLIES: These add their heat and distinctive flavour to many dishes. There are many different varieties and strengths of chilli. Your best bet is to have a selection to suit your taste and tolerance. Choose from the larger green ones, which are generally milder, to the fiery little red ones which will take the enamel off your teeth!

HERBS: Parsley is widely used in tapas. The flat-leaved Italian type is best. Other herbs which can be used regularly are oregano, basil, bay leaves and thyme. It makes sense to always have some of these in stock. If you've got a bit of mint in your garden, this can come in handy too for the Moorish-influenced dishes.

PAPRIKA: This is made from ground dried red peppers and comes in sweet (dulce) and hot (picante) varieties. It is used in many Spanish tapas dishes, adding its characteristic warmth, flavour and colour.

PEPPERS OR CAPSICUMS: From green to yellow to red, each is just a different stage of ripeness of the same fruit. Red ones are the most ripe and the sweetest flavour. They are cheap and last for ages in the fridge so there's no excuse for not having a couple at all times.

TOMATOES: Well-flavoured tomatoes should always be in your larder.

Improvisation

The important thing to remember is that nothing is set in stone as far as tapas is concerned. Use a bit of initiative and a bit of Spanish improvisation. And if you don't have a specific ingredient, try something else that's similar - you might just invent something special!

[3]

Egg & Cheese Recipes

Tortilla de Patatas (Spanish omelette)

THIS HAS TO BE the best-known tapas recipe of them all. Every Spanish tapas bar worth its name will have wedges of this on the menu.

Each region will have its own recipe. Some say it should be soft and others say it should be set hard; some say it should have onion and others say it should not; some serve it with mayonnaise and others serve it with tomato sauce.

I say just do it how you like it!

This delicious tapa can be served warm or cold.

Serves 4

1/2 pint of olive oil
350g (12oz) potatoes, peeled and sliced into 1cm (1/2in) slices
1 onion, sliced into rings
1-2 cloves garlic, crushed
4 eggs

Salt and freshly-ground black pepper
small handful of flat-leaf parsley

Par-boil the potato slices for about 5 mins. Drain and set aside. Heat the oil in a non-stick frying pan over a medium heat, then add the onion and the garlic. Cook until soft and translucent.

Add the potato slices and mix it all up a bit to combine. Put a lid on the pan and carry on cooking on a low heat for another 10-15 mins or until the potatoes are soft but retain a little 'bite'.

Beat the eggs and add the parsley, a good pinch of salt and black pepper to taste. Pour over the mixture in the pan and cook over a low to med heat until it's nearly set.

If you're good at it you can now toss it over and brown off the top. When I do this most of it goes on the floor so I just stick it under a hot grill for a couple of minutes to get the same effect.

You want it just set nicely and not like it came out of the Goodyear factory!

Serve it straight from the pan or allow it to cool and cut it into wedges on a plate. It's best savoured once it's cooled down a bit and the potatoes don't weld themselves to the roof of your mouth.

A little squeeze of lemon is a nice touch too.

Mediterranean eggs

Serves 4
   4 hard-boiled eggs
   50g (2oz) Roquefort cheese
   100g (4oz) pitted black olives
   1 tablespoon cottage cheese
   3 tablespoons olive oil
   A few leaves of the heart of a lettuce to decorate
   Mayonnaise

Shell the hard-boiled eggs and slice them in half lengthways. Save a few whole olives for decoration and finely dice the rest. Save a small amount of the diced olives as well.

Mix the hard-boiled egg yolks with the cheese, cottage cheese the diced olives and the olive oil. Stuff the eggs with this mixture. Put them on a serving dish, garnished with the lettuce leaves and whole olives, then sprinkle with the remaining diced olives.

Serve with the mayonnaise.

Manchego cheese

Manchego cheese is one of the simplest, original and classic tapas recipes. Just serve it with olives, crusty bread and a dry sherry (fino). A robust red wine (rioja) or a nutty Manzanilla sherry will also go well.

Manchego is also just as enjoyable as a dessert with fruit and/or a sweet sherry (cream or Xímenez). The best way to serve it is to cut a wedge out of the cheese, take the bottom bit of rind off, then cut it into triangular slices about 6mm (1/4") thick. Nothing fancy, that's it.

Huevos revueltos con jamon (Scrambled eggs with Serrano ham)

Scrambled eggs are a traditional tapa in Spain. This recipe uses serrano ham but you can use all kinds of ingredients to give it different flavours. Try it with bacon, chorizo, asparagus, spinach, mushrooms or onions.

50g (2oz) jamon serrano
1 tbsp olive oil (for frying)
4 eggs
2 tbsp milk (optional)
salt and pepper

Cut the jamon into small pieces. Beat the eggs together with the milk (if desired) and season with salt and pepper. Stir in the chopped jamon and pour into a frying pan. As the egg is cooking, gently stir it until it is cooked through but still very soft. Keep a close eye on it, if you leave it too long it will go like rubber! Once it's ready, get it on your plate straight away and serve with crusty bread. Tapas recipes don't come much simpler than this!

[4]

Fish & Seafood Recipes

Boquerones al vinagre (Anchovies in vinegar)

BOQUERONES are found in tapas bars everywhere. They are small, fresh anchovies (or whitebait) 'cooked' in vinegar and preserved with olive oil. They start out raw but the vinegar gives the flesh its cooked appearance.

They are, like their close relation the sardine, an oily fish stuffed full of proteins and minerals. I'm sure there must be loads of other good stuff in there as well, like Omega-3 acids, but I'm not a food scientist so don't take my word for it.

> ½ kilo (1lb) fresh anchovies
> 2 glasses white wine or sherry vinegar
> 4 tablespoons salt
> 1 glass water
> 2 or 3 garlic cloves, finely-chopped
> a handful of chopped parsley
> olive oil

Every region has its different methods but the basic principles are always the same for this tapas.

You'll need to use fresh anchovies. (Please don't confuse these with tinned or bottled anchovies, these will be far too salty and are not suitable for this dish.)

First you have to top and tail them, then clean and fillet the fish. This is a bit on the fiddly side as they're so small - but perseverance will be rewarded!

Rather than fillet them in the ordinary way, you can just slit them along the belly and open them out. This exposes the backbone which can be lifted out.

Next, you wash the fillets very well and pat them dry.

In a bowl, thoroughly mix the vinegar, water and salt, then test the mixture with one anchovy. Put it in the liquid and if it floats in the middle then the mixture is correct. If it sinks there is too much vinegar, if it floats there is too much salt.

When you've got it about right (don't be too fussy) you can add the remaining anchovies and cover the bowl.

The fish has to be left for one to two days in the refrigerator, soaking in the vinegar mixture. Again, this timing tends to vary, with some Spaniards just leaving them overnight.

The vinegar cleans and 'cooks' the fish and also softens any remaining little bones.

Once they are done, you throw the vinegar away and very carefully rinse off the fillets. Pat them dry again, cover them with good quality olive oil and add the chopped garlic to taste.

They will keep like this for quite a while so the garlic will infuse the flesh even more as they mature.

When you're ready to serve, simply put some on a small plate, sprinkle with some freshly-chopped parsley and serve with crusty bread to mop up the garlicky oil.

Or you can serve them on garlic-rubbed toast and let the oil soak in. They really are a flavourful little fishy tapas treat!

Boquerones fritos (Fried anchovies)

A lot of people don't like tinned anchovies but these are entirely different. Fresh anchovies are a real treat for fish lovers everywhere. And tapas doesn't come much simpler than this.

Serves 4

½ kilo (1lb) fresh anchovies
flour
salt
freshly-ground pepper
a couple of eggs (beaten)
olive oil (for frying)
1 lemon, cut into wedges

Take the heads and tails off, then gut the little fishes. You can then just slit them along the belly and open them out. This exposes the backbone which can be lifted out.

Next, you wash the fillets very well and pat them dry. This again is a bit fiddly but it's worth it.

Mix the flour, salt and pepper in a bowl. Heat the oil in a frying pan. Dip the fillets into the flour mixture, then into the beaten egg, and then into the hot oil quickly. Keep a close eye on them, they cook very quickly.

Serve straight away with the lemon wedges and crusty bread.

Calamares Fritos (Fried squid)

You can't go anywhere in Spain without coming across tapas recipes of fried squid. Forget the rubbery rings you may have experienced elsewhere on your travels, properly cooked, fresh squid is meltingly tender in the middle and crunchy and lemony on the outside. Do give it a go, but make sure your squids are fresh and that they didn't die of old age!

Serves 4

4 medium-sized fresh squids
3 tablespoons flour
½ teaspoon salt (or to taste)
freshly-ground black pepper
a couple of eggs, beaten
olive oil (for frying)
1 lemon, cut into wedges

To prepare and clean the squid, pull the tentacles gently away from the hood. This should bring out the intestines as well. Remove and discard the beak, cut off the tentacles from the gut and remove the soft bone from the hood. Wash the hood and tentacles under cold running water. Pull the skin away from the hood while doing this and discard it.

Cut the body into rings of about 1cm (½ inch) and the tentacles into bite-size pieces. Mix the flour, salt and pepper and coat the rings and tentacles in the mixture. Then dip them in the beaten egg and fry them in very hot oil until golden. Remove and drain on absorbent kitchen roll.

Serve with the lemon wedges and some extra seasoning if desired.

Gambas al ajillo (Garlic prawns)

Another example of how the simplest of tapas recipes can be so tasty. Don't use pre-cooked or frozen prawns for this dish, you need decent-sized fresh ones.

Serves 4

1 kg (2 lb) fresh prawns (shrimp)
6 or 8 cloves garlic, finely chopped
olive oil, for cooking

Pre-heat the oven to 250°C (500°F, gas 9). You can leave the heads on the prawns or take them off, it's up to you, but do peel them and leave the tails on. Carefully pull out the vein, starting at the head end.

Take four individual ovenproof dishes and put about 1cm (½ inch) of oil in each one.

Divide the chopped garlic beween them also and put them in the oven for 10 minutes or until they're sizzling hot.

Remove from the oven and divvy up the prawns into the four pots. Put back into the oven for another 5 minutes or so until the prawns are nicely pink and cooked.

Serve immediately, straight from the oven, while they're still sizzling. Don't forget to mop up all that hot, garlicky oil with some fresh bread.

Gambas pil-pil (Chilli & garlic prawns)

Now here we have a seriously flavourful, Moorish-inspired variation of the previous prawn recipe.

It is prepared and cooked in exactly the same way as the previous one except that you add some finely chopped fresh chillies (quantity according to your taste) at the same time as the garlic and oil before you heat the dishes in the oven.

Powerful stuff!

Ensalada de atun y huevos (Tuna & egg salad)

This is a very colourful tapas dish that you can throw together in no time. Although this is made with tuna and eggs, you can substitute almost anything you have in your refrigerator to make a quick and tasty salad.
Serves 4

2 medium tins of tuna, broken into chunks
2 eggs, hard boiled and segmented
1 red pepper, chopped into 1cm (½ inch) dice
1 green pepper, chopped into 1cm (½ inch) dice
black olives (for colour, but green will do), de-stoned and sliced
2 to 4 cherry tomatoes, chopped into small pieces
2 or 3 spring onions, sliced (or 1 small onion, chopped)
Extra virgin olive oil, a slosh or a glug to taste
Salt and pepper

Set aside the tuna and the egg. Take a large bowl and mix all the remaining ingredients. Season with the salt and freshly-ground black pepper, then glug in some of the oil and mix again to coat everything nicely. Arrange onto the plates, add the tuna chunks and egg segments, drizzle over a bit more oil and a grind of pepper and serve with some crusty bread. Instant tapas delight!

Pimiento asado y atun (Tuna & roasted red pepper)

Red peppers (or capsicums) are an extremely versatile vegetable. When slow-roasted or grilled they are an intensely sweet sensation. This tapas combination was just made for each other. If you're cooking for more people, just multiply the quantities.

Serves 2

1 can tuna, broken into largish chunks
2 red peppers
2 or 3 cloves garlic, thinly sliced
olive oil, for roasting
extra virgin olive oil, for dressing
half a lemon, for juice
salt and pepper

Pre-heat the oven to 180°C (350°F, gas 4). Cut the peppers into quarters lengthways, remove the seeds and the membranes. Place in a roasting pan, put the garlic slices on the peppers and drizzle liberally with the cooking oil. Roast for about 30 to 40 minutes, depending on the size of your peppers.

Keep an eye on them as you don't want them to burn at the edges. You also don't want the garlic to burn as this will make it bitter. If in doubt, it's safer to turn the heat down and roast them for longer.

When they're done, remove and let them cool down. Then cut the peppers into thin strips, arrange on a plate with the garlic and put the tuna on top. Squeeze some lemon juice over it and drizzle with the extra virgin oil.

A bit of salt, a grind or two of black pepper and you're in business. Don't forget the bread.

A variation is to grill the peppers. Just prepare them as above but without the garlic. Put them under the grill skin side up until the skin blackens, then put them in a plastic bag with the garlic slices to infuse and cool down. When serving you could use a red wine vinegar instead of the lemon juice.

For another variation, and more of a main meal, you could use fresh tuna steaks. Sear them in a hot frying pan but leave them pink in the middle, then serve with the roasted pepper still hot.

You could also sprinkle on some fresh herbs to taste. Thyme, parsley, oregano, dill - anything goes if you like it that way!

Atun y aceitunas con pan (Tuna and olive tapenade crostini)

Makes about 12

slices of bread (small baguette or similar, cut on the diagonal)
olive oil
a fresh tuna steak, about 250g (8oz)
Salt and pepper

For the tapenade:

a good handful of black olives, about 25, pitted
1 anchovy fillet
1 clove of garlic, roughly chopped
2 tablespoons extra virgin olive oil
a good few grinds of black pepper

Preheat the oven to 180°C (350°F). In a mixing bowl, toss the bread slices with the olive oil, salt and pepper, coating each side completely. Place the bread on a baking sheet and bake for about 6 to 8 minutes, or until crisp and slightly golden. Remove the bread from the oven and set aside. Season the tuna steak with olive oil, salt and pepper, then place on a hot grill plate or in a grill pan. Cook for about 2 to 3 minutes on each side for medium-rare or adjust timing according to your preference.

To make the tapenade, combine all of the ingredients in a food processor and puree for a few seconds, or until the mixture is smooth. This is just a guide, you can experiment with these amounts to suit how you prefer it.

To serve, slice the tuna into as many slices as you have bread, and place one slice on top of each crouton. Spread about a spoonful of the tapenade on top of each tuna slice. You can garnish it with some chopped chives or parsley if desired.

Buñuelos de bacalao (Salt cod fritters)

These little cod fritters originate from Catalonia and are made with salt cod. Originally introduced by Basque fishermen, salt cod has become a very popular tapas all over Spain. You need to soak the bacalao in fresh water for about 24 hours, changing the water a few times during this period. This will get rid of the excess salt.

Makes about 30

500g (1lb) bacalao (salt cod)
1 large potato, peeled
1 small onion, finely chopped
1-2 cloves garlic, crushed
30g (1oz) self-raising flour
2 tablespoons milk
50ml (2 fl oz)olive oil
2 eggs, separated
small handful flat-leaf parsley, chopped
olive or vegetable oil for frying

First of all, cook the potato for about 20 mins. until soft. Mash it with the milk and some of the olive oil then leave to cool.

While this is going on you can drain the cod and cover it with water in a pan. Bring to the boil then turn down the heat and poach it over a low heat for 30-45 minutes until soft and cooked. Remove and drain and when cool enough, remove the skin and any bones, then flake the fish into small pieces.

Heat the remaining olive oil and fry the onion until soft. Add the garlic and cook for a further minute or two.

Be careful not to overcook the garlic, there's nothing worse than burnt garlic for spoiling a dish.

Mix the potato, cod, onion/garlic, egg yolks, flour and parsley in a bowl, then whisk up the egg whites into a stiff consistency and fold into the mixture.

Fill a saucepan or frying pan to about 3-5cm (1-2in) and heat until med hot (200°C, 400°F) then drop in egg-sized dollops of the mixture. Cook until golden and puffed up. Drain onto paper towel and serve with lemon wedges.

Almejas con vino blanco (Clams with white wine)

Clams are a dish you will find all over Spain. There are different varieties of clam but for this tapas recipe just use the common 'carpet shell' ones. Many tapas bars serve the little baby almejas which are even more succulent. You won't find many dishes much simpler or more flavourful.

Serves 4

1 kilo of clams
2 large tomatoes
1 small onion, finely chopped
1 or 2 cloves garlic, finely chopped
about half a wine glass of white wine
a couple of grates of fresh nutmeg
olive oil for frying
flat-leaf parsley (about a half-handful)
salt and freshly-ground black pepper

Begin by soaking the clams in salt water for an hour or two to get rid of the grit, then rinse them under fresh water. Get rid of any that are open.

Next, score a cross in the tomatoes, place them first in boiling water for 30-60 seconds and then put them into cold water. Peel the skins off, quarter them and scrape out the seeds, then chop them finely.

Heat the oil in a large saucepan and fry the onions over a low heat until soft. Then add the garlic and the chopped tomatoes and cook for a further 5 minutes or so. Add the parsley, the nutmeg and season well with the salt and pepper

Add the clams and half a wine glass of water then cover with the lid and cook until all the clams have opened (check after about 5 mins.) Get rid of any that do not open.

Remove the lid, add the wine and cook over a low heat for about 4-5 mins to reduce the liquid. Don't stir the clams or they will fall out of their shells, just gently agitate the pan.

Serve immediately and pour the sauce over them, then just slurp them straight off the shells. And don't forget to get that crusty bread dipped into the tomatoey, garlicky, winey sauce!

Meat Recipes

Jamón Serrano/Iberico

THE ORIGINAL TAPAS recipe, and still hard to beat. Slice your ham into wafer-thin small pieces and serve on a plate. Make sure it's at a good warm room temperature and the fat is turning translucent. Some warm, toasted bread drizzled with extra virgin olive oil is all you'll need to make this an unforgettable experience.

Jamón Serrano with Almonds

Another very simple tapas recipe which can be prepared in an instant. First you heat a frying pan with a little olive oil in, then throw in a couple of handfuls of whole almonds. Give the pan a shake to evenly toast the nuts then sprinkle in some sea salt. You then place some slices of ham on a plate and top it all off with the still-warm almonds - seriously good!

Jamón, tomate y ajo con pan (Ham, tomato & garlic bruschetta)

Can you make toast? Two more minutes and you've got these next two delightful tapas.

slices of bread (baguette or similar, cut on the diagonal)
1 clove garlic, cut in half
1 very ripe tomato
slices of jamon serrano
extra-virgin olive oil

Preheat the grill. Toast the bread and, while still warm, rub with the cut end of the halved garlic to flavour them. Then rub the bread with the halved tomato to squeeze in as much of the flesh as you can. Sprinkle with a pinch of salt and some freshly-ground pepper, drizzle with some extra-virgin olive oil and top it off with the ham.

Jamón y queso tostadas (Grilled serrano ham and manchego cheese bruschetta)

slices of bread (baguette or similar, cut on the diagonal)
slices of jamon serrano
slices of manchego cheese
extra-virgin olive oil
whole-grain mustard (optional)

Preheat the grill. Toast each slice of bread on one side only until lightly golden brown, then turn over and drizzle with the olive oil. Place the cheese slices on the bread, top each slice of cheese with a slice of ham and grill until the cheese begins to melt. Serve with the mustard separately or you can spread it on the cheese before it goes under the grill.

A variation on this is to lightly toast both sides of the bread first and rub one side with half a clove of garlic before you drizzle the oil and place the cheese and ham. Just make sure the whole slice is covered or you could end up with the toast edges burnt to a crisp!

Albóndigas (Meatballs in spicy tomato sauce)

Another of the staple tapas recipes which you will find everywhere. This is a dish which originated with the Moors so you will usually find some exotic spices in most recipes, especially those from the Andalucian region where the Moors had the most influence.

Serves 6

For the meatballs:

150g (6oz) minced pork
150g (6oz) minced veal (or beef)
3 cloves garlic
50g (2oz) breadcrumbs
1 egg
1 teaspoon cumin powder
1 teaspoon ground coriander
1 teaspoon ground nutmeg
1 pinch cinnamon
salt and pepper
olive oil, for frying

In a bowl, mix together all the ingredients (not the olive oil) until you have a nice stiff consistency. Cover and leave in the fridge for about half an hour. When ready, make your meatballs, taking about a tablespoon of mixture for each one. Heat about a tablespoon of oil in a frying pan and fry the meatballs in batches on a med-high heat. You want them nicely browned. Add more oil if necessary for each batch. Drain on some kitchen roll and keep warm.

For the sauce:

1 onion, chopped
1 clove garlic, finely chopped
1 400g (16oz) can chopped tomatoes
3 to 4 teaspoons tomato puree
½ teaspoon cayenne pepper
125ml (4 fl oz) dry white wine
125ml (4 fl oz) chicken stock
100g (4oz) frozen peas (or fresh peas)
freshly-ground black pepper
1 tablespoon olive oil

Use the same frying pan (but tip out any excess fat) to make use of the lovely meat juices that should have caramelised on the bottom. Add the oil if necessary and cook the onion until soft and translucent, then add the garlic, a few grinds of black pepper and cook for another minute or so. Make sure you don't burn the garlic as it will taste bitter. Add the wine and increase the heat to high, let the wine boil for a minute or so to intensify the flavour. Add the can of tomatoes, the puree and the stock. Bring back to the boil then simmer for about 10 minutes. Add the peas, stir in the cayenne pepper and the meatballs and continue simmering for another 10 minutes.

Serve it up, piping hot, straight from the pan with plenty of crusty bread to mop up the sauce.

Croquetas de Jamón (Serrano ham croquettes)

These melt-in-the-mouth little croquettes are very popular tapas with the Spanish. You will, again, find them just about everywhere. You can use any number of different fillings but, for me, you just can't beat jamón. Try it with prawns, hard-boiled egg, salmon, cheese or vegetables.

Serves 6

100g (4oz) jamón serrano, finely chopped
1 onion, finely-chopped
100g (4oz) unsalted butter
150g (6oz) plain flour (100g for cooking, 50g for coating)
150ml (5 fl oz) whole milk
150ml (5 fl oz) chicken stock
salt and pepper
1 pinch of nutmeg (if desired)
2 eggs, beaten
50g (2oz) breadcrumbs
olive oil, for frying

In a saucepan, heat the butter over a low to med heat, then add the onion and a couple of grinds of black pepper, cook until the onions are soft (do not brown). Stir in 100g of the flour and cook until the mixture is almost dry and starts to change colour.

Remove from the heat and add the milk very gradually, stirring constantly to prevent lumps. When you've got a smooth mixture you can add the chicken stock, put back on the heat and let it boil to thicken it up.

Keep that stirring going and remember what I said about exact quantities. It's better to hold back a little while adding the liquids and judge the correct thickness. You can always add more if it's too thick but you've got an awful lot of boiling to do if it's too thin!

Once you've got a nice thick mixture, add the ham and taste for seasoning. Add a little salt if necessary but don't overdo it, the ham will give it a salty bite. For an optional flavouring, you could also add a pinch of nutmeg at this stage. You can now leave this for a couple of hours in the refrigerator to help it set. If you wish, you can leave them overnight.

Prepare the coatings by putting the extra 50g of flour, the 50g of breadcrumbs and the beaten egg into three separate bowls. Take about a tablespoon of the cold mixture and roll it into a croquette shape. Dip it first into the flour, then into the egg, then into the breadcrumbs.

When you've prepared all the croquettes you need to put them back in the fridge for half an hour. When you're ready to cook, fill the oil to about 5cm (2in) in a good saucepan and heat to about smoking point. It needs to be good and hot. You can then start frying them in batches. They'll only take 2 to 3 minutes a batch until nicely crisp and golden. Remove, drain and place on kitchen roll in a warm oven until they're all done.

Serve hot while they're still crunchy on the outside and meltingly smooth on the inside. One of those recipes which makes tapas so special!

Empanadas de Cerdo (Pies of pork!)

Empanadas are basically pies. You can make a whole one in a pie dish and cut it into segments, or make them into little pasties or parcels. I prefer the little individual ones, it seems to fit in with the idea of tapas better.

This tapas recipe is for minced pork and roasted peppers but you can make them with minced beef or lamb, fish and seafood or vegetables. Or a combination of whatever takes your fancy!

You need to make about 500g (1lb) of pastry. I will assume you know how to do this. If not, any good cookbook will show you how. Bear in mind that you want a light, crumbly mixture so just cut the liquid in and don't knead it.

Makes about 20

500g (1lb) of pastry
250g (1/2lb) of pork loin, minced
1 tsp. paprika
olive oil for roasting and frying
1/2 tsp. oregano
2 onions, chopped
1-2 cloves garlic, chopped
3 tomatoes, peeled, seeded and chopped
1 tsp. tomato puree
small handful chopped flat-leaf parsley
Salt and pepper
2 or 3 large red peppers, roasted and chopped
1 egg, beaten

Pre-heat the oven to 180°C (350°F, gas 4). Cut the peppers into quarters lengthways, remove the seeds and the membranes. Place in a roasting pan and drizzle liberally with some olive oil. Roast for about 30 to 40 minutes, depending on the size of your peppers.

Meanwhile, heat the oil in a frying pan and fry the onions until soft and translucent. Add the garlic and cook for another minute or two. Raise the heat and add the minced pork to brown it through.

Then add the paprika, oregano, tomatoes, puree, parsley and salt and pepper to taste. Stir it all together and cook for a further 5-10 minutes to get all those flavours going. At the last minute, add the chopped roasted pepper and combine.

Increase the heat of the oven to 190°C (375°F, gas 5) then roll out half the pastry very thinly so that you can cut about 20 rounds of 10cm (4in) diameter. Repeat with the other half.

Fill each round with a heaped tablespoon of the mixture and fold over into a pasty, brushing the edges with water and pinching them to seal them.

Place them on a lightly-oiled baking tray, brush them with the egg mixture and bake for about 30 mins. or until golden. Serve hot or cold.

Garbanzos y chorizo (Chickpeas & chorizo()

This hearty dish is again inspired by the Moors who introduced the chickpea or garbanzo. This is a very common tapas dish now found throughout Spain. It is best cooked using the 'picante' (hot) style of sausage to give it a fiery little Moroccan kick.

Serves 6

175g (6oz) dried chickpeas
350g (12oz) chorizo, diced into cubes about the same size as the chickpeas
1 onion, finely chopped
1 clove garlic, chopped or crushed
2 tbs olive oil
750ml (1.3 pints) chicken stock
1 bay leaf
1 pinch dried thyme
3 or 4 cloves
1 stick of cinnamon
1 tbs flat-leaf parsley

Cover the chickpeas with water in a bowl and leave to soak for 12 hours or so. Drain and place in a large saucepan with the bay leaf, cloves and cinnamon stick. Add the stock and enough water to cover the peas completely. Bring to the boil then reduce the heat and simmer until the peas are tender. This should take about an hour but keep an eye on them, you don't want them to go mushy and you don't want them to boil dry. Add more water if necessary during this period. Drain and remove the herbs and spices.

Meanwhile medium heat the oil in a frying pan, add the chopped onion and cook gently until translucent. Add the garlic and thyme and cook for about a minute then turn up the heat a bit and add the chorizo. Cook for about three minutes then add the chickpeas and mix it all up thoroughly. Cook for just long enough to heat it all through. The oil from the sausage will turn it all a lovely red colour. Remove from the heat and stir in the parsley.

This is one of those tapas recipes that needs very little, if any, seasoning but if you feel you must, you can add salt and/or pepper after you've tested and tasted it. I prefer it hot but you can enjoy it just as well cold.

[6]

Vegetable Recipes

A WORD OF WARNING: Although these are vegetable recipes, they are not *vegetarian* recipes. Be aware that there may be some meat or meat stock included here.

Olives a la Sevillana

Those olives again! The following couple of simple and tasty olive tapas recipes are perfect for your evening appetiser. With most olive recipes you can use pitted olives or whole (stone in) olives. I think that whole olives are generally better because they retain their texture and 'bite' better. You do, of course, have the stones to contend with so if you prefer, use pitted ones.

250g (8oz) large green olives

1/2 teaspoon ground cumin

1 teaspoon fresh oregano

1 teaspoon fresh rosemary

1 teaspoon fresh thyme

1/2 teapsoon dried thyme

2 bay leaves

1/2 teaspoon fennel seed

2 teaspoons crushed black pepper

4 cloves garlic, lightly crushed and peeled

4 anchovy fillets, chopped

50/50 mix of white wine vinegar and water

Find a glass jar big enough to take all the olives and the marinade. Sterilise the jar with boiling water and leave to dry naturally in a warm oven (don't use a tea towel).

Lightly crush the olives and place in a bowl with all the other dry ingredients. Mix it all up thoroughly.

Fill the jar with the olives, then add the vinegar and water mix.

Shake well and marinate at room temperature for several days. They should be eaten at room temperature but will keep for weeks in the refrigerator.

Chilli Olives

You can make this tapas recipe with green olives, black olives or cured (wrinkled) olives. Each will have a different flavour to tempt you with.

500g (1lb) olives
3 cloves garlic, thinly sliced
a good handful flat-leaf parsley, chopped
1 tablespoon chilli flakes
3 teaspoons coriander seeds, crushed
2 teaspoons cumin seeds, crushed
500ml (1pt) strong-flavoured olive oil
2 tablespoons white wine vinegar

Soak the sliced garlic in the vinegar for 24 hours then drain and discard the vinegar.

In a bowl, mix the garlic with the rest of the dry ingredients and the parsley.

Sterilise a 1 ltr. (1.75 pints) jar with boiling water and leave to dry naturally in a warm oven (don't use a tea towel). Place the olives in the jar and fill up with the olive oil. Give it a gentle shake to mix the ingredients and then marinade for one to two weeks. Serve at room temperature.

They'll keep for a month or two in the 'fridge (if you can leave it that long!) but don't forget to get them out an hour or two before you need them to let them acclimatise.

Patatas Bravas (Crispy potatoes in a spicy tomato sauce)

Patatas bravas is a simple and traditional tapas recipe which is a mainstay in almost every tapas bar you come across. As with the tortilla, each bar will have its own recipe, and each will tell you that theirs is obviously the best!

You can get a good idea of the quality of a tapas bar by sampling their Patatas Bravas. The potatoes should be crisp on the outside but still firm on the inside and the sauce should be rich, glossy and spicy.

Serves 4

1 kg (2 lb) potatoes, peeled, and cut into 2cm (1in) inch cubes

1 small onion, finely chopped

2 cloves garlic, crushed

Salt and freshly ground black pepper

500g (1lb) good tomatoes

3 teaspoons Pimentón (paprika)

1/4 teaspoon cayenne pepper

1/4 teaspoon chopped fresh thyme

1 teaspoon tomato puree or tablespoon ketchup

Chopped flat-leaf parsley, to garnish

1 cup (8 fl. oz) olive oil, for frying

Once cut, rinse the potatoes and dry on some paper towel. Heat the oil in a frying pan to about 180°C (350°F) and cook the chunks of potato for about 5 minutes (or until lightly golden) in small batches. Drain on paper towels and set aside.

Meanwhile, prepare the tomatoes by cutting a cross in the base and plunging them into boiling water for 10 to 15 seconds. Plunge into cold water and the skin should peel away easily. Chop the tomatoes.

Heat some more oil in a saucepan and fry the onion until soft. Add the garlic, paprika, thyme and cayenne pepper then cook for another couple of minutes until it all smells fragrant and spicy. Add the chopped tomato, the puree or ketchup and cook, uncovered, until the sauce thickens. This should take about 20 minutes.

While this is cooking, add the salt and pepper to taste. If the sauce looks like it's getting too thick, add some water. It should be a thick sauce though, you don't want it too runny and making your potatoes soggy.

While the sauce is simmering you can re-heat the frying oil and re-fry the potatoes. This gives them an even crisper coating and prevents the sauce from soaking in too much.

Another way to prepare the potatoes, and one which I prefer, is to par-boil them for 5 to 10 minutes first. Then drain the water, let the steam evaporate for a minute or so and then give the pan a good shake. This roughs up the outsides nicely.

When the sauce is nearly ready, fry the potatoes only once in the hot oil and serve immediately. You will find that this gives them a beautifully crisp outside and a soft and fluffy inside. Just like my mum used to make!

To serve, place the potatoes in a serving bowl, season them if desired, then cover with lashings of spicy sauce. Sprinkle some chopped parsley all over it and tuck in!

Ensalada rusa (Russian salad)

Another tapas recipe that you'll find everywhere. This is a very quick and simple recipe that you can throw together in no time.

1 or 2 large potatoes
100g (4oz) young green beans
2 eggs
tin of tuna
green or black olives, pitted (some chopped)
mayonnaise (home-made or Mr Hellman's!)
salt and freshly-ground black pepper
sqeeze of fresh lemon juice

Peel the potatoes and cut into small dice of about 1cm. Boil in salted water for about 10 mins or until soft. Drain and leave to cool

Hard boil the eggs then remove the shells and leave in cold water to cool. When they're cool enough to handle, chop into cubes and place in a bowl with the potato.

Blanch the beans and refresh in cold water to retain their 'bite'. Then add these and the chopped olives to the bowl. Finally, add the tuna, the mayonnaise, the salt and pepper and the lemon juice and mix gently to combine.

Garnish with the whole olives, maybe some flat-leaf parsley and serve.

There are many variations on this dish. Some have carrots, or peas, or capers, or anchovies, or red pepper (capsicum), or mustard - or a combination of all the above!

Try it all and see what suits you best.

Croquetas (Croquettes)

These melt-in-the-mouth little croquettes are very popular tapas with the Spanish. You will, again, find them just about everywhere. You can use any number of different fillings. Try it with hard-boiled egg, cheese or vegetables. This recipe is exactly the same as the Jamon Croquetas recipe in the meat section. Just leave out the jamon.

Serves 6

1 onion, finely-chopped

100g (4oz) unsalted butter

150g (6oz) plain flour (100g for cooking, 50g for coating)

150ml (5 fl oz) whole milk

150ml (5 fl oz) vegetable or chicken stock

salt and pepper

1 pinch of nutmeg (if desired)

2 eggs, beaten

50g (2oz) breadcrumbs

olive oil, for frying

In a saucepan, heat the butter over a low to med heat, then add the onion and a couple of grinds of black pepper, cook until the onions are soft (do not brown). Stir in 100g of the flour and cook until the mixture is almost dry and starts to change colour.

Remove from the heat and add the milk very gradually, stirring constantly to prevent lumps. When you've got a smooth mixture you can add the stock, put back on the heat and let it boil to thicken it up.

Keep that stirring going and remember what I said about exact quantities. It's better to hold back a little while adding the liquids and judge the correct thickness. You can always add more if it's too thick but you've got an awful lot of boiling to do if it's too thin!

Once you've got a nice thick mixture, taste and adjust for seasoning. For an optional flavouring, you could also add a pinch of nutmeg at this stage. You can now leave this for a couple of hours in the refrigerator to help it set. If you wish, you can leave them overnight.

Prepare the coatings by putting the extra 50g of flour, the 50g of breadcrumbs and the beaten egg into three separate bowls. Take about a tablespoon of the cold mixture and roll it into a croquette shape. Dip it first into the flour, then into the egg, then into the breadcrumbs.

When you've prepared all the croquettes you need to put them back in the fridge for half an hour. When you're ready to cook, fill the oil to about 5cm (2in) in a good saucepan and heat to about smoking point. It needs to be good and hot. You can then start frying them in batches. They'll only take 2 to 3 minutes a batch until nicely crisp and golden. Remove, drain and place on kitchen roll in a warm oven until they're all done.

Serve hot while they're still crunchy on the outside and meltingly smooth on the inside.

Beautiful!

Champiñones al ajillo (Garlic mushrooms)

There are not many tapas recipes more Spanish than this. Gorgeous mushrooms infused with the exotic flavours of spices, olive oil, garlic and Spanish Sherry.
Serves 4

50ml (2 fl.oz) good, strong olive oil

250g (8 oz) mushrooms, sliced or quartered

4-6 cloves garlic, sliced, chopped or minced to taste

3 tablespoons dry sherry

2 tablespoons lemon juice

large pinch of dried chilli flakes

large pinch of pimenton (paprika)

Salt and freshly-ground black pepper

handful of chopped parsley, to garnish

Heat the oil in a frying pan or skillet and fry the mushrooms over high heat for 2 to 3 minutes, stirring constantly. Lower the heat to medium and add the garlic, lemon juice, sherry, salt and pepper.

For a milder flavour you can leave it at that if you like. But if you like a bit of 'fireworks', now's the time to add the dried chilli and paprika as well.

Cook for another 5 minutes or so until the garlic and mushrooms have softened then remove from the heat, sprinkle with chopped parsley and divide up into pre-heated 'little dishes'.

Serve with plenty of fresh, crusty bread to mop up those seriously-garlicky juices.

Champiñones al pimienta (Peppered mushrooms)

This is a simple variation on the previous tapas. Handy if you're going out on a hot date and don't want to overpower your partner with your breath!
Serves 4

250g (8oz) mushrooms
50ml (2 fl.oz) olive oil
1 small onion, diced finely
salt
lots of freshly-ground black pepper
chopped parsley

Heat the olive oil in a frying pan and fry the mushrooms and onion over a medium heat until they are getting soft. Add the salt and pepper and cook for a further couple of minutes. Serve as above.

Almendras (Fried almonds)

This has to be one of the simplest, tastiest and quickest ways to serve up some tapas when unexpected guests come a-knockin'. I am never without a pack almonds in the cupboard. Quantities really don't matter here, just use what you've got!

> whole blanched almonds
> olive oil
> sea salt

Heat up a little oil in a frying pan. Throw in the almonds and shake around until golden brown all over. Be careful not to burn them, though. Remove and drain them onto paper towels then put them into a large bowl.

Sprinkle liberally with the salt, give 'em a good shake and dig-in with your fingers while they're hot. Don't be too polite though, or there won't be any left!

Roasted Spicy Almonds

Another way to serve almonds but with a spicy Moorish influence. Again, just use whatever you've got in the cupboard.

whole blanched almonds
1/2 tsp cayenne pepper
1/2 tsp pimentón (paprika)
1 tsp cumin
knob of melted butter
olive oil
sea salt

Preheat the oven to 180°C (350°F). Combine all the other ingredients and toss in the almonds, giving them a good coating. Place them in a single layer on a baking sheet and roast until golden brown (about 10 to 15 minutes but keep an eye on them, you don't want them black!). Serve hot or cold.

Deep-fried Aubergine with Honey

There are few sights more appealing than a display of perfect, deep purple aubergines. It makes you just want to buy a few and try something out. This recipe is a simple and tasty way to prepare them with a hint of Moroccan influence. You will need one large fruit per two people.

Aubergines cut widthways into 1cm (½") slices
3 to 4 units plain flour
1 unit cumin powder
1 unit baking powder
Cold water
Salt and pepper
Olive or sunflower oil for frying
A good clear honey for pouring over

Heat the oil in a deep-fat fryer or large saucepan.

To make the batter, mix the sifted flour, cumin and baking powder in the ratio above to coat however many aubergines you have. Add the salt and pepper then add just enough water to make a very stiff batter. (A tip here is to leave out the baking powder and use carbonated water instead. This gives the same light and crunchy finish once cooked.)

Coat the slices of aubergine well and drop them straight into the very hot oil. Cook for a few minutes until they are golden brown and crisp then remove with a slotted spoon and drain on some kitchen roll. Serve on a plate straight away with a generous coating of the honey.

[7]

Origins & Regions

THE ORIGIN OF TAPAS is the subject of many an argument in the local bar. (It seems to depend on which area of Spain you are from!) It is said that the first tapa was simply a hunk of bread which was placed over the glass to keep the flies out. Hence the word 'tapas' was born. Tapa literally meaning 'cover' or 'lid'.

Another theory is that unscrupulous bar owners would try to mask the taste of their bad wines by giving slices of strong cheese to their customers. There are many more theories but whatever the truth is, there is no doubting that tapas have now become an established part of world cuisine - and quite rightly so.

Originally these small snacks were given free to anyone who bought a drink in the bar but now you will nearly always have to pay for them.

In the beginning somewhere must have been the olive - plain and simple, on its own. What better accompaniment to a glass of dry fino sherry? Or perhaps some almonds; fried in olive oil, sprinkled with salt and served while they're still hot? These are the original tapas; the simplest of foods, requiring little or no preparation.

As the tradition developed, tapas became more of an elaborate event, with each region developing their own specialities. They were still 'little dishes' but the personalities of thousands of bar owners over the years have stamped them with the identities they have today.

A very brief history

Age-old regional methods and local ingredients have been influenced throughout the country's long history by the incorporation of many ingredients and influences from different cultures and countries.

The east coast was invaded by the Romans, who introduced the olive and irrigation methods.

The invasion of the Moors also brought olives to the south, as well as almonds, citrus fruits and fragrant spices. The influences of their 700 year occupation remain today, especially in Andalucia.

The discovery of the New World brought with it the introduction of tomatoes, sweet peppers (capiscums), chilli peppers, beans and potatoes. These were readily accepted and easily grown in Spain's ideal micro-climates.

Regions and influences

Spain's landscape is extremely diverse and covers areas such as mountain ranges and dusty plains, olive and fruit groves plus fertile orchards and rich arable lands.

Spain also has climate extremes. Regions that are cold and wet, regions that are hot and dry, and just about everything in between. It has a huge coastline, facing both the Atlantic ocean and the Mediterranean sea.

Spain's fishing industry is one of the most active, and pro-active, in Europe. Hardly surprising then, that the cuisine of its coastal regions is very heavily based on fish and seafood.

The **Basque** province has both wonderful fish and seafood from the Atlantic ocean and some of the finest cattle, sheep and dairy foods in Spain. Portions are large, as is to be expected in a cold climate, but the cooking has a certain refinement.

Dishes cooked al chilindrôn, in a flavourful sauce based on the particularly good local red peppers, and tomatoes, onions and garlic, are typical of **Navarra** and **Aragon**. Trout from the clear mountain streams that rise in the Pyrenees are a regional favourite, especially cooked with ham.

The food of **Catalonia** is exciting and richly varied and features interesting sauces, such as romesco and Allioli, aromatic herbs and noticeable similarities with French Mediterranean food, such as Zarzuela, a close cousin of bouillabaise.

Valencia and **Murcia** form one of the most densely populated and richest agricultural areas of Europe, and exhibit distinct Moorish influences. Here there are groves of orange and almonds, large market gardens and rice fields. The last two provide the ingredients for authentic Paella Valenciana - the addition of fish and shellfish is a modern adaptation that has become universally popular.

Andalucia is the land of olives, olive oil and sizzling fried foods, particularly the varied sea and shellfish from around the long coastline.

In contrast, **Extremadura** is a land of tough, hardy countrymen, and simple hearty cooking with many stew-type dishes.

The vast exposed **Central Plain** produces Spain's most well-known cheese: Manchego, as well as many other sheeps' milk cheeses. The area is most generally thought of as a land of roasts, principally young lamb and suckling pigs.

Galicia and **Asturias** are renowned for the quality of their fish and shellfish, and is the home of excellent empanadas. The climate is comparatively cold and wet, so appetites tend to be hearty and the local dishes correspondingly warming and filling. Locally produced cider is popular for drinking and also for using in cooking.

THANK YOU!

Thank you for buying this book and for reading this far, I really do appreciate it.

If you have one or two minutes more to spare, you would be doing me a huge, *huge* favour by leaving an honest review where you bought it.

Each one of these online reviews plays an important part in spreading the word to other readers, and can help greatly towards a book's visibility to other searchers.

I hope this book has inspired you to try some of the many easy and mouthwatering traditional tapas recipes available today.

The best way is to just get stuck in, open a bottle or two, invite some friends over and enjoy your tapas the Spanish way.

Thank you once again, and I wish you good fortune and happiness, wherever you may be.

Salud!

ABOUT THE AUTHOR

Stephen Lean is a writer, website designer and Spanish food nut. He spends his time between the UK and Andalucia, southern Spain, which has allowed him to discover more about Spain, its people and the Spanish way of life.

He has been fortunate enough to meet some lovely people and sample some pretty outstanding local food.

He is the creator and webmaster of Google's top-ranked tapas website: www.Proper-Spanish-Tapas.com.

If this book has tickled your tapas taste buds you can connect with Steve and find out *"Everything there is to know about Tapas, the small plate with the BIG flavour"* by visiting his website.

NOTES

Printed in Great Britain
by Amazon